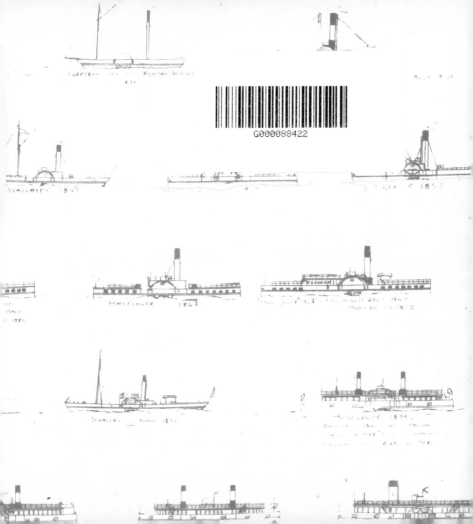

CROSS THE MERSEY

850 YEARS OF THE FAMOUS MERSEY FERRIES

by
Arabella McIntyre-Brown
Guy Woodland

garlic
PRESS

CROSS THE MERSEY

850 YEARS OF THE MERSEY FERRIES

Written by Arabella McIntyre-Brown
Photography by Guy Woodland
Cover design: Ken Ashcroft
Proofreader: Debbie Woodland
Printed and bound in Spain by Bookprint SL

ISBN 1-904099-03-3

First published in 2003 by Garlic Press Publishing Ltd
71 Prenton Road West, Birkenhead, CH42 9PZ
Tel +44 (0)151 608 7006
www.garlicpress.co.uk

Acknowledgements

Our thanks to everyone at Mersey Ferries who helped us get the
book from an idea to publication, and special thanks to:
Layton Quinton
Sue McGrath
Annette Cain
Captain Dennis Titherington
Captain Dave Langton
Mate Colin Potter
Peter Thompson

Thanks also to Mike Edwards at Kaleidoscope, and to the following
for allowing us to use images:
Photographs on p30, 62, 82 courtesy of Stuart Rayner
Postcards on p13, 34, 44 courtesy of Ian Boumphrey
Other material from the Mersey Ferries archives p21, 22, 24, 25, 27,
28, 29, 39, 44, 46, 47, 48
The Gordon Ditchfield collection p45
Steve Dodd at *big*cheese for his help with the end papers and
the digital origination learning curve

As always, our gratitude to a splendid team of colleagues and
friends whose talent, expertise and enthusiasm make our job so
much easier.

CROSS THE MERSEY

850 YEARS OF THE WORLD-FAMOUS FERRIES

Captain Dennis Titherington went to work on the Wallasey Corporation's ferry service as a deckboy in 1961. Today he is Mersey Ferries' Marine Superintendent, in charge of the vessels and their operations.

A passenger asked me the other day whether I ever got bored of Liverpool and the ferries. Bored? This is my home town – I was born in Everton and although I've seen many beautiful places in the world, I couldn't think about living and working anywhere else.

What better job could there be than this? To be given the privilege of helping to run the world's oldest and most famous ferry service; to get to know this great river in all its moods; to watch the city I love grow and evolve; to work with and for the people of Merseyside.

In my working life with the Mersey's ferries, I've seen the best of times and, for the ferries and the city itself, the worst. When I started work in 1961, Liverpool was the most exciting city to be in; it was on the brink of being ... what did Alan Ginsberg call it? ... 'at the centre of human consciousness'. Today Liverpool is nicknamed the capital of cool; we are bidding for European Capital of Culture and being proposed as a World Heritage Site.

The 1970s and 1980s were not so good in Liverpool; the ferries were under threat and we had some narrow times. But when I look back at what we have achieved, the only regret I have is that I don't have another 40 years to go at the Ferries.

Enjoy this terrific book; and come back to see us again... and again.

the story

There have been boats on the Mersey for as long as people have lived here: since the Neolithic Boat People settled here about 4,000 years ago.

The Romans may have been the first to use a ferry to cross the river, as remains of Roman roads have been found in Birkenhead and Otterspool.

But the first known ferry service was provided by the monks of Birkenhead Priory, founded in 1150AD by Hamon de Masci, Baron of Dunham. The Benedictine monks would row over to the little fishing village of Liverpool on market days, and would offer the service to travellers. In 1318 Edward II allowed the Priory to provide board and lodging for travellers waiting for good weather to cross the river, and on 13th April 1330 his son Edward III confirmed the royal charter to operate the ferry. This made the Birkenhead-Liverpool ferry a royal highway, still marked today by the crown on the gangway posts at Woodside and Pier Head.

Edward III also granted the right to the Earl of Chester to run a ferry from Seacombe to Birkenhead, establishing the Wallasey ferry; these two operations remained separate until they were merged as Mersey Ferries in 1968.

In the 738 intervening years, ownership of the ferries changed hands many times, in the early days at the whim of the king. In 1545, after the dissolution of the monasteries, Henry VIII sold the Priory, and its ferry rights were granted to Sir Ralph Worsley. His descendants sold the rights in 1833 to Liverpool MP John Cleveland; his heirs sold the ferry rights in 1842 to the Birkenhead Commissioners.

There were several other private ferry services upstream of Birkenhead: the first Tranmere ferry lease was granted by the Crown to John Poole in 1586; Rock Ferry was in existence by 1709 and by 1774 there was a coach service between Chester and New Ferry.

The New Brighton and Egremont ferry was established by James Atherton in 1830 to serve the new resorts; in 1850 it was bought by Edward Coulbourn who sold it in 1860 to the Wallasey Corporation.

Today all the ferry services operate under the single banner of Mersey Ferries, part of Merseytravel.

Rowing across the Mersey would take 90 minutes in calm weather; much longer in rough conditions

In 1229 there is the first record of a Liverpool ferry, being leased to the burgesses of the town

The Liverpool rights to a ferry were sold at auction on 17 May 1544

Birkenhead ferry, 1800

crew

A far cry from the days when passengers were rowed across by a monk, the ferries now have quite a crew on board and on shore to carry up to 800 passengers across the river in comfort and safety.

On shore, there are staff on the information and ticket desk, in the shops and cafes at each terminal, and the backstage team in the offices at Seacombe and Pier Head. Down on the landing stages the stage-men help folk on and off, check tickets, tie up the boats, manoeuvre the heavy gangways, and cast off.

On board, the crew members the passengers mostly see are the two seapersons and the catering assistant; below decks is the chief engineer and, on *Woodchurch*, the second engineer. Up on the bridge are the captain and the mate; the mate's main duties are as helmsman and assisting the captain in berthing the vessel; he is also the liaison between captain and crew, looks after bridge management, stores and so on, and is the first aider on board. It takes at least two years' working as a deckhand, learning the ropes and acquiring seaperson's skills before being considered for a mate's ticket, and another two years before getting the chance to try for a master's river ticket.

In one day the ferry has over 100 arrivals and departures on the Liverpool-Wirral service

14

Captains Jimmy Vass (right) and Derek Penton on the bridge of *Royal Daffodil*

On weekdays the ferry's day begins at 7.35am with the first departure from Seacombe to Liverpool; until 10am the ferry runs a triangular shuttle service between Seacombe, Pier Head and Woodside, taking ten minutes to travel across the river and getting commuters to work in the time-honoured way.

At 10am the first river cruise leaves Pier Head, taking a leisurely 50 minutes for the round trip taking in some of the sights up and down river on the way. At 4.15pm the service reverts back to the commuter shuttle until the last ferry leaves Pier Head at 7.15pm. The service starts a little later on weekends and bank holidays, the first ferry leaving Seacombe at 9.05am.

The crew has two day shifts, changing over at 2pm, when the captains confer about the morning's events and sailing conditions. At the end of the day's service, the night crew comes on board; a half crew of one from the bridge, one from the deck and one from the engine room, the night crew cleans and maintains the boat and is on hand to deal with any emergencies.

To a layman, it might look an easy job to chug back and forth across a river, but as one of the captains said, handling a ferry on the Mersey is 'like driving a bus on ice'. Some 500 tons weight, manoeuvred across one of the strongest tidal flows in Britain, cutting across the path of other river traffic and giving way to everything from dinghies to 350,000 ton tankers, with no traffic lights, no lanes, and no brakes.

The safety of passengers is of paramount importance

Even for a captain with a lifetime's experience, a combination of tide and wind can make it extremely tricky to berth the vessel, especially at Seacombe, the narrowest point on the river.

So if you see photographs of celebrities 'steering' the ferry, you can be sure that it was taken while the boat was safely tied up at the landing stage. No room for amateurs on Mersey Ferries!

landings

Woodside's Victorian visitor centre is a listed building, complete with an old tram on show inside. The terminal itself was built in 1985

Before the Ship Canal opened, ferries also ran to Ellesmere Port and Runcorn, although it was not a regular service

Piers and landing stages were for ever being damaged by storms, collisions and even fire. In 1907 a very severe gale damaged New Brighton's landing stage which floated off and had to be rescued

There are now three ferry terminals in normal use: Liverpool Pier Head, Seacombe (Wallasey) and Woodside (Birkenhead). But at one time or another there were 11 ferry points on the Wirral shore: New Brighton, Egremont, Seacombe, Woodside, Monk's Ferry, Birkenhead, Tranmere, Rock Ferry, New Ferry, Eastham and Ellesmere Port.

The slipway first used by the 14th century monks of Birkenhead Priory was known as Monk's Ferry until it was last used in 1878. Tranmere started as the crossing point to Birkenhead until the pool was filled in; it was revived in the 1800s but closed in 1904.

New Brighton, Egremont, New Ferry and Eastham all began in the 1800s when the Wirral became a popular dormitory and resort for Liverpool. During the Garden Festival in 1984, Mersey Ferries ran an extra service to Otterspool on the Liverpool shore.

In the early days, passengers would get their feet wet getting in and out of boats, or pay the ferryman to carry them; later on slipways or wooden stages were used, then wooden or iron piers, and eventually floating landing stages, which allowed passengers to embark easily at any point on the tide.

Imagine having to scramble in and out of boats over mud and shingle

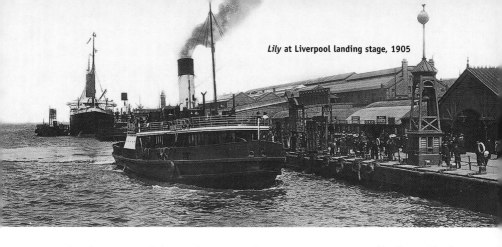

Lily at Liverpool landing stage, 1905

On the Liverpool shore, the terminal at the Pier Head is the latest evolution of the ferry terminal; back in the days of rowing and sailing boats, ferries would run up on to the Strand; later there was a pier built out from the Old Dock, and when George's Dock was first built, ferry passengers had to get ashore via dangerous, narrow steps cut into the dock wall. When the floating landing stage was built, combining stages for the ferries and the Princes Dock liners, it was half a mile long: the world's longest floating structure.

Even the floating landing stages can be defeated by the winds and tides; it is getting on and off the ferry, rather than the crossing itself, that can force suspension of the service in exceptionally bad weather.

The Liverpool landing stage was burned down in 1874; a penny ballad included the lines: 'The poor Cheshire people looked most awful black/They came oe'r the ferries but couldn't get back/And one cranky Welshman got nearly smoke-dried/ Looking out for the steamer for Birkenhead side'

It's a tonic WALLASEY CORPORATION FERRIES

ROYAL IRIS

Dance Cruises ♪

(BARS and BUFFETS)

DANCE CRUISES . . .
throughout New Brighton

FERRY SERVICES

Between **SEACOMBE** and **LIVERPOOL**

Every ten m...

Until 1886, when the railway tunnel was opened, the Mersey ferries were the only means of getting people, animals and vehicles across the river without the 40-odd mile trek round by Warrington.

Each year, as well as millions of foot passengers, cyclists, horse-drawn carts and drays, carriages, even stage coaches were carried across the river on board the ferries, and in 1879 the first purpose-built luggage boat joined the Birkenhead service.

Even when the first road tunnel was opened in 1934, horse-drawn vehicles, steam-driven lorries, and vehicles carrying hazardous freight were prohibited, and had to continue to use the luggage boats. It was only in 1947 that the last vehicle-carrying ferry service ended; now bicycles, dogs and hand-luggage are taken on board, but no horses, thanks.

The ferries were never just for getting from A to B; excursions, pleasure trips and cruises have been part of the service for at least 150 years. Excursions out to the Bar, trips to see visiting ships or watch regattas and firework displays, works outings or birthday dos on board with a band and a bar – the Mersey ferries lead a double life as popular party boats and hard-working public transport.

New Brighton was a hugely popular local destination. In 1953 the ferries carried 2,907,000 to that resort alone

On Whit Monday 1918, some 93,000 passengers took the Liverpool-Birkenhead ferry

The Mersey was a must for visiting royalty including the Shah of Persia, the Sultan of Zanzibar and the Amir of Afghanistan, as well, of course, as the British royal family

When the Channel Fleet visited in 1863, some 55,000 people were ferried out to see the Navy ships

In 1864 the Rock Ferry steamer Wasp *went to the rescue of the ship* Lottie Sleigh *which, laden with 11 tons of gunpowder and anchored in the river, caught fire.* Wasp *rescued the crew just before the ship exploded, breaking every window on the waterfront on both sides of the river*

I t is tricky enough negotiating the Mersey on a good day, with its tides, sandbanks, and other shipping; but up to the 20th century the ferries could be vulnerable to all sorts of hazard, natural and otherwise.

Ferrymen rowing passengers the 90-minute journey across river often overloaded boats, and would rook naive passengers with extortionate charges.

Worse yet - at one stage passengers were at the mercy of river pirates; one traveller complained that in the middle of the river he had been robbed of his money, his horse and his lady.

Believe it or not, the Wirral coastline was second only to Cornwall for wrecking - wreckers would use false lights during bad weather to lure ships on to the

Rough weather at Birkenhead

"GEM" 1861

rocks near New Brighton, then ransack the ship and hide the booty in caves and tunnels along the shore.

As well as the criminals, there were the criminally stupid, like the captain of the steamboat *Rothesay Castle* in 1831 whose 'mental aberration due to intoxication' sank the boat and drowned those aboard.

In 1798 two men were killed by a cannon shot fired as a greeting to the town by a homeward-bound vessel. Liverpool afterwards imposed a £10 fine on any ship saluting the town.

Collisions were common, mostly in fog or at night, like the two boats in 1834 returning from a boxing match near Rock Ferry; both boats were capsized with up to 50 lives lost. Some years later the Seacombe ferry *Gem* collided with the sailing ship *Bowfell* in dense fog and several people were drowned.

Before radar was installed in 1947, ferry captains had to rely on fog bells to give them an audible target to aim for. When Liverpool, Seacombe and Woodside all had mechanically operated bells, the fog bell at New Brighton still had to be rung manually - once a minute while the fog lasted. The lanyard ran from the bell to the stageman's bunk

The Mersey Ferries were the first in the world to install a radar system for safe navigation in fog, in 1947. At first the radar operator at Seacombe would have to radio information to the ferry captains, but later all the ferries were fitted with radar scanners

In the 1960s, the last boats back from New Brighton would be jam-packed. Captain Titherington recalls that 1,000 passengers crowding towards the gangway to get off at Pier Head would make even these very stable ferries keel over about two feet

Fire was another hazard; in 1899 the Catholic reform ship *Clarence* burned down to the water's edge; the Birkenhead ferry steamers *Mersey* and *Firefly* rescued 235 officers and boys.

Quite beyond control was the weather; Liverpool's archives are full of tales of storms doing terrible damage to life and property; early in 1793 not only was there a 'perfect hurricane', but a gale in which the Frodsham market boat capsized and killed 17, and the privateer *Pelican* sank at Seacombe with 70 drowned. Storms still hit the Mersey: Force 9 is common, and, in 1976, a hurricane sank the new stage at Pier Head.

In 1956 a watchman thwarted an attempt to scuttle the *Royal Daffodil*

But today's ferries are remarkably stable vessels with a superb safety record. The only danger to passenger safety now is a bad storm making the landing stages 'a bit lively', as Captain Titherington puts it. If passengers can't safely get on and off the ferry, the service is suspended even if the ferries can still cope with the conditions on the river.

On board radar shows the helmsman everything on the river at all times, so he no longer has to listen for the old fog bell; although the bells still ring in fog.

Modern construction and technology aren't always proof against wind and tide. The exceptional force of the 1976 hurricane washed away the new landing stage at Pier Head

crisis

How little ticket prices changed in 700 years...
In 1357 the charge for a foot passenger was a halfpenny, for a man and a horse 1d, for a man with a laden horse 2d.
In 1848 ferriage from Liverpool to Wirral was reduced from 2d to 1d.
In 1952 a cheap evening ticket to Seacombe was 4d

Between 1870 and 1949 five ferry points closed for one reason or another, leaving Liverpool, Woodside, Seacombe and New Brighton. The opening of the world's first underwater railway in 1886 and the line's electrification in 1903 was predicted to be the ferries' doom, but in 1919 the Seacombe ferry alone carried 22 million passengers.

It wasn't until the Mersey road tunnel opened in 1934 that serious damage was done to the ferries' business and even then car ownership was a fraction of today's numbers. It was after World War 2, when car ownership, foreign holidays, labour mobility and a marked rise in the standard of living saw the decline in the numbers using the Mersey ferries.

The luggage boats were redundant and finished in

1947, and the enormous flow of traffic through the road tunnel meant a second Mersey tunnel opening in 1971 (the year that the New Brighton ferry closed).

The Birkenhead and Wallasey ferry operations had been merged into Mersey Ferries at the end of 1968, under the aegis of the Mersey Passenger Transport Executive.

The 1970s saw massive changes across Merseyside and the start of terrible economic decline. In 1977 a bill was put before Parliament to discontinue ferry services altogether but it failed to get support and the Mersey ferries survived the crisis.

By the 1980s, however, it was clear that the ferries couldn't sustain themselves on commuter traffic any more, but it was unthinkable that the Mersey should be without its famous ferry fleet. After asking passengers for their views, and with the growing tide of tourists coming to Liverpool, Merseytravel relaunched the ferries as a heritage and visitor attraction in 1990.

Merseytravel immediately invested £5 million in Mersey Ferries: refurbishing *Mountwood* and *Woodchurch*, upgrading the terminals and adding new attractions such as the aquarium, extending off-peak runs to 50-minute cruises, and running special excursions and events throughout the year, all against the world-famous backdrop of Liverpool's fabulous waterfront.

The Clippers starting
their round the world
race in October 2002

Since 1990, Mersey Ferries has carried more than nine million passengers, of which about 30% are commuters taking advantage of the ancient royal highway to get to work every morning.

The fleet of *Woodchurch*, *Royal Daffodil* and *Royal Iris of the Mersey* continues the honourable tradition of mixing business with pleasure. Acting as a tender for the great visiting liners such as the *QEII*, taking passengers into the thick of things during the annual River Festival, the Tall Ships and Clipper Races, fireworks nights and so on. Merseysiders, with salt water in their veins, love any excuse to be messing about in boats, after all...

Mersey Ferries won Visitor Attraction of the Year in 1996 by Merseyside Tourism Board

The ferries have a role to play with schools, touching on curriculum subjects from history and geography to biology, environment, and social studies.

The parties go on, too. Mersey Ferries themed cruises include jazz, salsa, blues, Beatles, glam rock, 60s and 70s music; there are daytime cruises up the Manchester Ship Canal, out into Liverpool Bay, and in search of the Mersey's rich and protected wildlife.

The splendid new addition to the Seacombe terminal will be the Space Centre, due to open in 2004. Linked with the astrotelescope project at Liverpool John Moores University, and using special effects, state of the art technology and live links across the globe, the Space Centre will give visitors the chance to take control of some of the biggest robotic telescopes positioned around the world. Watch special astronomical events and get the latest news on space; or go back on a sensational ride on the Time Machine to the very beginning of the universe

By the late 1800s steam ferries were stable and powerful enough to consider carrying railway carriages across the Mersey, but the plan failed for lack of a suitable terminal on the Liverpool side. The underwater railway tunnel was built instead, in 1886

The Mersey ferries have developed through four main stages to do, mostly, with how they were powered. The first boats were rowed by the monks, and later by any oarsman with the strength to row the 90-minute crossing and carry passengers between boat and shore. Records from 1357 show that ferry tolls allowed for laden and unladen horses, so the boats cannot have been mere dinghies.

Sail boats began to be used, eventually fully rigged sailing ships, but despite being faster and not reliant on muscle power, they were even more at the mercy of the winds. So travellers could be delayed for days

The paddlesteamer *Claughton* in 1880; Queen Victoria took a trip on this ferry in 1886

by bad weather and probably wished they had opted for the long route via Warrington.

It was in 1815 when the ferries made their technological quantum leap. The first steam ferry on the Mersey was an odd craft called the *Etna*; consisting of two hulls each 65ft long with a paddle wheel in the middle and a deck 25ft wide, *Etna* was very awkward to steer and not very stable: an uncomfortable ride for passengers. Still, *Etna*'s arrival meant the ferry service could run to a timetable for the first time, and a second paddlesteamer, *Vesuvius*, soon arrived.

By 1840 all ten ferry services across the Mersey were using paddlesteamers. The next major improvement was in 1864: saloon ferries with large, bright cabins above deck rather than cramped, gloomy and badly ventilated space below deck.

The first coal-fired screw steamer, *Crocus*, came in 1884; her sister *Snowdrop* in 1885; twin-screws *Mersey* and *Wirral* joined the Woodside service in 1890. The ferries went from strength to strength, carrying increasingly heavy loads, even after the opening of the Mersey road tunnel. The ferries had switched fuels from coal to oil, but it wasn't until 1949 that the Mersey had its first diesel-powered ferry. The last steam ferry on the Mersey was the *Wallasey*, which sailed for the last time at Whitsun, 1963.

Despite having Cammell Laird's shipyard right next door, the ferries were not all built on the Mersey. Launched on rivers from the Dart to the Tay, ferries came to the Mersey from shipyards the length and breadth of the British Isles.

The Mersey proves a valuable testing ground for innovative naval architecture and engineering; ferries on this river have to be tough, powerful, stable, efficient and very manoeuvrable.

The 1920s and 1930s generation of steam powered ferries were successful designs, with clear links to today's familiar shapes. *Thurstaston* and *Claughton*, for instance, were 150ft long with a beam of 41ft, carrying up to 1,433 passengers. Their triple expansion steam reciprocating engines delivered 1,300 horsepower and a speed of 11 knots. The contract for the two ships was £85,690.

The old Birkenhead steamers had tall funnels and no superstructure on their large upper deck. There was no navigating bridge; captain and first officer had only a small central wheelhouse or side cabs - not much protection against the worst of the Mersey weather.

Two Wallasey ferries, *Wallasey* and *Marlowe*, were built on the Tay by Caledon Shipbuilding & Engineering

Cammell Laird built all five of the Birkenhead ferries that made up the post-war fleet. Upton, Hinderton, Thurstaston, Claughton and Bidston were built on the Mersey between 1925 and 1933

The template for 20th century Mersey ferries was the Wallasey ship *Rose*, in 1900

The 1927 ferries Wallasey and Marlowe were good-looking, popular and efficient, carrying up to 2,233 passengers and using nine tons of coal per day, steaming at 12 knots

Company of Dundee and delivered to the Mersey in the summer of 1927. Slightly bigger than their Birkenhead counterparts, *Wallasey* and *Marlowe* were 151ft long and 48ft broad, taking 2,233 passengers and steaming at 12 knots. They were more manoeuvrable than their predecessors, due to the new Flettner system of twin rudders, and more fuel-efficient.

In 1949 Wallasey experimented with a motor launch: the *Channel Belle* (later renamed the *Wallasey Belle*) built in 1944 as a Navy rescue launch, and converted by Bolsons at Poole for passenger use. She could carry only 250 passengers, at 108ft long and 126 tons, so was used for the much quieter night shift. Too small for cruising, she was really not cut out for the vagaries of the Mersey and, after four years, was sold.

Of Wallasey's four 1950s diesel ferries, it was the *Royal Iris* that stood out, having a very different shape to the others and being more than twice the tonnage.

Leasowe (1951) and *Egremont* (1952) were each 566 gross tons, 145ft long with a 34ft beam; licensed to carry 1,470 passengers (692 when cruising). Powered by two Crossley two-stroke 1,280 horsepower diesel engines, the two ships made about 14 knots. The *Leasowe* was said by several ferry masters to be the easiest of all the ferries to handle.

The cost of building ferries had leapt in 20-odd years since the last steamers were built; *Royal Iris* cost the Wallasey Corporation £300,800 in 1951; the following year *Egremont* cost £144,500, and *Royal Daffodil II* cost £282,160 in 1958.

Mersey Ferries once experimented with a high speed twin-hulled catamaran, Highland Seabird, in 1982. The cat was certainly fast across the river, but lost too much time in the swell at the landing stages, especially between Woodside and Seacombe. She was also not up to the fierce Mersey winter weather

The two main trends in naming ferries split between Birkenhead and Wallasey. Birkenhead chose local place names such as *Woodchurch* and *Claughton*, while Wallasey picked flowers. The style of lettering on the bows was different, too: Birkenhead used italic script, while Wallasey went for capitals.

The very first steam ferry, in 1817, was *Etna*, shortly followed by *Vesuvius*. The Rock Ferry boats were insects: *Ant*, *Bee*, *Wasp*, *Mayfly* and *Firefly*.

Sometimes there was confusion between ferry companies: in 1873 there was a ferry called *Birkenhead* at Tranmere, and another *Birkenhead* running from Woodside; on 30 July the two steamers collided.

There have been four *Merseys*, four *Birkenheads*, and three *Woodsides* and *Bebingtons* in the fleet

Two Wallasey boats in 1927 were named after chairmen of the ferries committee - *Francis Storey* and *J Farley*. Both men died before the vessels were delivered; each ferry wore a painted four-inch wide purple mourning band for their first year.

The other distinction between Birkenhead and Wallasey, of course, was the funnel colours: black and red for Birkenhead, black and white for Wallasey.

The Eastham service's main ferries were Pearl, Ruby and Sapphire, *built in 1897 and run till the ferry closed in 1929*

Wallasey's flower ferries included:
Water Lily *1862*
May Flower *1862*
Wild Rose *1862*
Heather Bell *1863*
Sunflower *1879*
Daisy *1879*
Primrose *1880*
Violet *1883*
Crocus *1884*
Snowdrop *1884*
Thistle *1891*
Shamrock *1891*
Pansy *1896*
Tulip *1898*
Rose *1900*
Lily *1901*
Iris *1906*
Daffodil *1906*
Bluebell *1910*

Commander Valentine Gibbs, skipper of the Iris, *was one of 472 men injured; 176 men died*

Eleven Victoria Crosses were awarded for bravery in the Zeebrugge raid

A commemorative service for the Zeebrugge raid is held every year on a Mersey ferry, on the Sunday nearest to St George's Day

In 1906 Wallasey took ownership of what would become their most famous ferries: *Iris* and *Daffodil*. They were normal ferries until 1918, when they were requisitioned by the Admiralty to take part in a raid on Zeebrugge on St George's Day, 23 April.

The Zeebrugge and Ostend Canals were the route for Germany U-boats to reach the English Channel, so blockships were to be sunk to stop them. The ferries (chosen for their light draught and strong framing) were to land a storming party of Royal Navy men and Marines to take the gun battery at the harbour mouth.

At a minute past midnight, *Iris* and *Daffodil* went in with *HMS Vindictive* against intense enemy fire, and lay for an hour being shelled and strafed, while the blockships were sunk across the channel.

Iris and *Daffodil* escaped, just - both ferries were terribly damaged and had to be helped home. Battle-

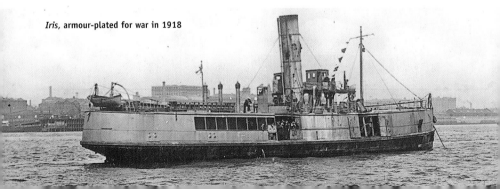

Iris, armour-plated for war in 1918

During WW2 the Wallasey luggage boat *Liscard* was fitted with cranes to offload heavy cargo

scarred, they returned to the Mersey for a major refit before returning to normal ferry duties.

In recognition of their courageous part in the raid, King George V granted Wallasey Corporation permission to add the 'Royal' prefix to both names.

During World War 2, *Royal Daffodil II* (built in 1934) acted as a tender and troopship as well as continuing the vital ferry service; when an air-raid warning sounded, she was on standby at the Pier Head in full steam, ready to unload a troop ship anchored in the Mersey if it was bombed.

Ironically *Royal Daffodil II* took a direct hit while tied up at Seacombe, on 8 May 1941 (during the May Blitz). It wasn't until June 1942 that she was salvaged.

When Royal Daffodil *was bombed, the only casualty was a stoker who was blown out of the engine room and lost his false teeth*

300 tons of silt and sand had to be removed from Royal Daffodil *before she could be refloated, refitted and returned to ferry service in June 1943*

In 1985, to promote Merseyside, Royal Iris *sailed right round the south coast, up the Thames and under Tower Bridge, where she berthed next to* HMS Belfast *for a month. The 1,500 mile trip was quite a challenge for the aging ferry, but she made the same trip – one way only – in 1991*

Royal Iris's nicknames were 'the fish and chip boat', 'the booze boat' and 'the love boat'

The second Royal Daffodil II *was delivered to the Mersey the day that the author was born, on 20 April 1958*

There have now been four ferries called *Royal Daffodil*, three called *Royal Iris*, and one named *Royal Iris of the Mersey*. The original 'royal' boats, built in 1906, survived till the 1930s.

Royal Daffodil II was built in 1934 and lasted till 1962 when she was towed away with *Claughton* for scrapping. The Liverpool Echo carried a sad photograph of ferryman Keith Smith waving goodbye to the two ferries from the New Brighton landing stage.

Royal Iris II was built in 1932 and had the most elaborate interior of any ferry to date, and the first to have three decks with awnings on the sundeck. She was renamed *St Hilary* in 1950, and was sold in 1956.

Her successor was the famous and distinctive yellow and green *Royal Iris*, delivered on 28 April 1951. The largest and most spacious ferry built for the Mersey, she was 1,234 tons, 160ft overall length and 48ft in the beam; she could carry up to 2,296 passengers.

For 40 years *Royal Iris* was a party boat: how many people flocked on board to drink, dine and dance the night away? She was a popular day cruise ship too; the white and blue livery she had for the Garden Festival in 1984 she kept till the late 1980s.

On 21 June 1977 the Queen and Prince Philip boarded *Royal Iris* for the Jubilee Mersey Review; in 1990 *Royal Iris* attended another visiting Queen - the *QEII*.

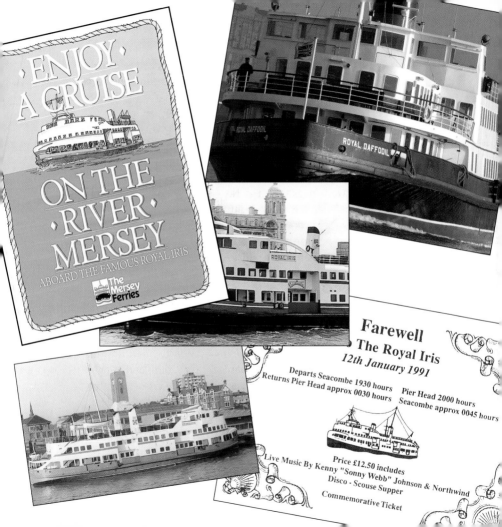

ENJOY A CRUISE ON THE RIVER MERSEY

ABOARD THE FAMOUS ROYAL IRIS

The Mersey Ferries

ROYAL DAFFODIL

ROYAL IRIS

Farewell
The Royal Iris
12th January 1991

Departs Seacombe 1930 hours
Returns Pier Head approx 0030 hours

Pier Head 2000 hours
Seacombe approx 0045 hours

Price £12.50 includes
Live Music By Kenny "Sonny Webb" Johnson & Northwind
Disco - Scouse Supper

Commemorative Ticket

During Prohibition in America, Bermuda was a haven for drinkers, attracting booze cruises. The ferry boat taking passengers ashore was none other than the former Mersey ferry Woodside, which sailed to Bermuda under its own steam in 1930

Ferries often had a change of career once their Mersey days were over; they were usually renamed and many were rebuilt so they became virtually unrecognisable.

Ireland was a common destination, with the original *Royal Iris*, *John Joyce* and *Francis Storey* all going to Cork; the *Lily* went to Dublin and became the *Failte*, sailing on the Liffey for many years.

The *Perch Rock* had one of the longest careers of all the Mersey ferries. A Wallasey luggage boat built on the Tay in 1929, she sailed on the Mersey till 1953 when she was sold for £8,800 to a Swedish company,

was renamed *Betula* and converted into a freight train ferry to carry sugar beet. In 1954 she turned to car carrying and later became a passenger ferry again, operating for Linjebuss between Helsingborg and Helsingor as the original ship of the Scandinavian Ferry Line. In 1971 she was sold to AB Skanska Cementgjutenet of Malmo and was converted for use as a cement platform. A versatile vessel!

The 1951 *Leasowe* left the Mersey in 1974, went to the Greek islands as *Naias II* and in 1980 was rebuilt as the *Cavo Doro*; she was last seen in a Morocco dry dock, waiting to be sold. *Royal Daffodil II* followed *Leasowe* to Greece in 1977 as the *Ioulis Keas II*.

One ferry still to be seen is the 1952 *Egremont*, which is moored, minus engines, in picturesque Salcombe Bay on the south Devon coast, as the club house of the Island Cruising Club.

The much-loved 1950s 'love boat', *Royal Iris*, waved an emotional farewell to the Mersey in 1991. Her last cruise was on 12 January; at midnight, crew and passengers joined hands to the strains of *Ferry 'cross the Mersey*. On 21 April that year *Royal Iris* carried 600 people on the 73rd anniversary trip to commemorate the Zeebrugge raid of 1918. She was sold that November for use as a floating nightclub, and now lies berthed in London, by the Thames Barrier.

The *QEII* visited the Mersey for the first time on 24 July 1990 to mark the 150th anniversary of Cunard's founding in Liverpool; 2003 is the *QEII*'s final transatlantic season before the launch of the *Queen Mary II*

Today's Mersey ferry fleet consists of three boats: *Woodchurch, Royal Daffodil*, and *Royal Iris of the Mersey*. They were, however, all Birkenhead ferries originally: the two 'royal' ferries started life as *Overchurch* and *Mountwood*.

In 1960, the Birkenhead and Wallasey fleets were still running independently under the aegis of the two Wirral corporations (they merged into Mersey Ferries in December 1968). The Birkenhead fleet consisted of the old steamships *Thurstaston, Bidston* and *Claughton* while Wallasey had a modern fleet; apart from the 1927 steamer *Wallasey*, the diesel powered *Leasowe, Egremont* and the queen of the river, *Royal Iris*, were all less than ten years old, and *Royal Daffodil II* had only been in service since 1958.

Hard to imagine the Mersey without these unmistakable ferry shapes

In spring of 1960 Birkenhead took delivery of its two new diesel ferries, *Mountwood* and *Woodchurch*, and commissioned *Overchurch*, which was launched two years later; it is these three ferries which make up today's fleet.

By the end of 1963 the last of the old Mersey steam ferries had gone: it was the end of an era.

Each ferry holds 35 tons of fuel in its tanks and burns a ton in 12 hours: so a Mersey ferry could travel across the Atlantic to New York (and half way back, actually) without refuelling

Overchurch was the most recent Mersey ferry to be built, launched at Cammell Laird's yard in 1962

Although the current ferries were built to carry 1,200 passengers, they are now licensed to carry 860 for their daily service, and 396 for longer cruises

Wallasey's diesel-powered fleet has now all gone: Leasowe *was sold in 1974 and* Egremont *in 1975;* Royal Daffodil II *was withdrawn from service in 1977.* Royal Iris *was the last Wallasey ferry on the Mersey, in service for 40 years until 1991*

Birkenhead Corporation commissioned *Mountwood* and *Woodchurch* in 1957 from Philip & Son near Dartmouth, Devon – the yard which had built *Leasowe* and *Egremont* for Wallasey.

Birkenhead's new ferries were based on the same design, both 152ft long overall, with a beam of 40 feet and 464 gross tons; the three decks could hold 1,200 passengers on the top promenade deck, in saloon accommodation fore and aft on the main deck, and a buffet/smoke room below.

The eight cylinder engines by Crossley Bros of Manchester drove twin screws and developed almost

With a speed of 12 knots on a six-knot tide, the ferries can reach up to 18 knots

1400bhp. Crossley's developed special air brakes and a servo for the ferries so the captain could stop and reverse the main propulsion units quickly from the bridge, increasing manoeuvrability and safety.

Mountwood was launched into the Dart on 6 July 1959; *Woodchurch* on 29 October 1959; they were fitted out and delivered to the Mersey in 1960.

In 1962 Birkenhead's third diesel ferry was delivered; built on the Mersey at Cammell Laird, the *Overchurch* was similar to her Dart-built sisters, but was the first of an all-welded construction and a bit larger: six inches longer and four tons heavier.

All three ferries' original livery was Birkenhead's black and red; in 1984 they were all were given new livery of red white and blue for the Garden Festival, while the old Royal Iris was painted white and blue.

Woodchurch *was
taken out of service
early in 1981 and
laid up at Morpeth
Dock until 1983*

*Since the name
Royal Iris is still
used by the old ferry
berthed in London,
we have* Royal Iris
of the Mersey

*By 1989 the ferries
were running at an
annual deficit of
£2.5 million; a new
strategy was agreed,
focusing on tourism
and heritage rather
than traditional
commuter traffic.
£12 million was
earmarked to
upgrade the ferries,
the terminals and
the landing stages*

After two threats to the ferries' existence, in 1977 and the late 1980s, Merseytravel committed itself to major investment in the Mersey's 850 year-old transport service. *Woodchurch* and *Mountwood* had already been taken out of service for major refurbishment and engine repairs at Mannings Marine in Bootle.

The two ships were virtually rebuilt with much improved accommodation for passengers and crew; meanwhile *Overchurch* operated the new triangular service on her own. *Woodchurch* and *Mountwood* made a much-heralded return to service in 1990 in time for the *QEII*'s first visit to the Mersey on 24 July.

In November 1998, *Overchurch* went into dry dock in Manchester and emerged as the Mersey Ferries' new flagship, *Royal Daffodil*. Her conversion included new engines, new saloons the full width of the ship on the main deck, a dance floor below and full dining facilities for parties of up to 350 people.

Mountwood went into dry dock in March 2001 for her own conversion, and was renamed *Royal Iris of the Mersey* on her return in April 2002.

So the Mersey's royal sisters are back at last, and with the faithful *Woodchurch*, the three of them continue a service tradition of carrying people on this most famous of rivers, that dates back over eight centuries, and looks ahead for many more.

chapter 3

the river

Geography

In about 2000BC, the Liverpool area was marshland and forest stretching for miles along a big lake that extended from Warrington to Formby. A primeval forest of oak, pine and birch stretched from Freshfield across to the top of the Wirral; the engineer Stephenson believed that an earthquake created the estuary some-time around 400AD

It's hard to imagine the River Mersey without the Pier Head, and that is less than 100 years old; think how this stretch of river must have looked 400 years ago before the docks were built.

The river was much wider, lapping up against the wall of St Nicholas's Churchyard and on the sandy beaches exposed at low tide. A map of Liverpool in 1650 shows the river sweeping into a Sea Lake (extending from Chavasse Park to the Baltic Fleet pub) that narrowed into the Pool, under a bridge (roughly where the Moat House hotel is) and along what is now Paradise Street and Whitechapel to the Queensway Tunnel entrance. On the Wirral side, there were two main inlets: the wide Wallasey or Bidston Pool and the narrow Birkenhead Pool.

New Brighton is right at the river mouth, where the Mersey flows into Liverpool Bay and the Irish Sea. The

Mersey may be associated with Liverpool but it begins in Stockport, at the confluence of the Rivers Goyt and Tame; it runs a 70-mile course to the sea, joining the Manchester Ship Canal for a short stretch. Below a weir near Warrington the Mersey is tidal, with the second highest tidal range in the UK (after the Severn), varying each month from 4m at neaps (lowest tide each month) to 10m at spring tides: ie between high and low tide the river can rise and fall by 30ft.

The strong tide creates deep channels and sandbanks; combined with often fierce winds and weather, this makes the Mersey no place for amateur sailors. While the big ships have pilot boats to guide them in, the ferry captains must know the river's features intimately: Pluckington Bank, Devil's Bank, Sloyne Roads, the Middle Deep (40ft deep at low water), Garston and Eastham Channels, the Duke's Buoy (known locally as John Wayne's Lad) and so many others that it takes many years to learn. And the river is never still - channels and sandbanks shift over time, and tides can be whipped up by the prevailing north-westerly wind or a wicked south-easterly straight off the Irish Sea.

But weather these days is meek and mild compared to the old days, when frequent and terrible storms or dense fogs could last for days and do dreadful damage to property and shipping.

The Queen's Channel was first charted by Captain William Gill (1795-1858), first captain of the Isle of Man Steam Packet Company's ships

The name Mersey is linked to the ancient kingdom of Mercia, and comes from the word maere, *meaning border (same root as the Welsh marches)*

Liverpool harbourmaster William Hutchinson kept tidal records; between 1768 and 1793; he noted the height and time of every high water, which allowed him to calculate and publish the first tide tables for mariners

wildlife

Until the 17th century, fishing was the main sub-sistence activity for folk living on the shores of the Mersey, and until pollution began to take its toll it was a river teeming with life. But a combination of the Mersey's shape and urban development killed off almost everything for more than 100 years.

In tidal rivers with a wide mouth, the tides flush the estuary twice a day and wash pollution out to sea. The Mersey, though, is wide between Widnes and Liverpool (where several canals join the river), and narrows at its mouth, between New Brighton and Seaforth; so pollution tends to wash around in the river and build up heavily polluted sediment.

The industrial revolution in the 18th century and the

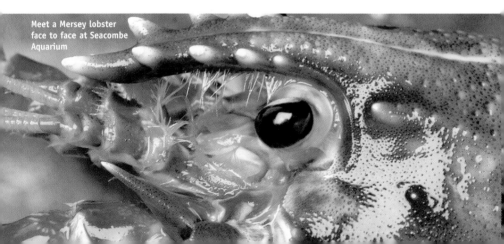

Meet a Mersey lobster face to face at Seacombe Aquarium

explosion of population in and around Liverpool and the Wirral meant that industrial waste and raw domestic sewage was discharged into the Mersey in staggering quantities until the river was foul, evil-smelling and poisonous to wildlife (and humans).

In 1980, however, a massive clean-up campaign began, and over £550 million has been spent; a 27-mile interceptor sewer stops sewage from entering the river and environment legislation has made industry more responsible. The Mersey is still rated Class 3 (too polluted for large fish populations) but the pollution levels are dropping, the fish are coming back, and the river should be upgraded to Class 2 by 2010.

The Mersey may still be a long way from its pre-industrial best, but the fish and marine mammals are

The Mersey estuary has two SSSIs (sites of special scientific interest); along with the Wirral coast and the sandhills of Formby Point, this is a natural area of enormous importance. Even in the heart of the docks, the Seaforth Nature Conservation Centre attracts thousands of nesting and migrating birds

Cormorants – real life Liver Birds – are
back on the Mersey at last

coming back in significant numbers.

In the winter, anglers now fish for cod from small boats anchored off Seacombe; plaice, dabs, sole and sea bass are regular catches. From the ferry you can often see shoals of grey mullet feeding off algae on the landing stage supports, and for the first time in well over 100 years, a salmon was caught in the Mersey in 2001. Octopus, too - even a swordfish.

Marine mammals are more visible from the ferry decks, of course. Look for grey seals in the summer basking around the landing stage at Woodside; harbour porpoises and bottle-nosed dolphins are seen now and then in the river, and a Minke Whale swam upriver as far as Runcorn and had to be rescued.

Sea birds have followed the fish back – cormorants race the ferries over the water, and in the winter the air is full of screaming birds - common, lesser black, herring and black-headed gulls. At low tide, look for oystercatchers, redshank, dunlin, curlew and occasionally a whimbrel. Swans nest in Waterloo and Princes Docks, as do mallard; great crested grebes, teal and shelduck visit, as do brent and canada geese.

Right by Pier Head you can see goldfinches, skylarks, wagtails, mistle thrushes, blackbirds, linnets, whitethroats, blackcaps, willow warblers, and others. An urban desert? Hardly! Just keep your eyes open.

At the aquarium at Seacombe ferry terminal visitors can come face to face with some of the creatures that live in the Mersey, from the metre-long conger eel to starfish, sea-anemones and transparent shrimps

With binoculars, you might see a pair of ravens around the Anglican Cathedral, where they nested in 2000

Buzzards, kestrels, sparrowhawks and peregrines can be spotted occasionally; a pair of peregrines nest on the tunnel vent at Woodside, easily seen from the deck of the ferry

In the early 1700s the River Weaver was made navigable by Thomas Steers (who built Liverpool's first dock) to get salt from the Cheshire mines via the Mersey to Liverpool's refineries and docks; in the 1720s work began to widen the Mersey above Runcorn to get barges up to the River Irwell and into Manchester, and in 1755 Liverpool dock engineer Henry Berry began work on the Sankey Canal to bring coal from Lancashire pits to fuel Liverpool's growing chemical industries. The Bridgewater Canal also linked Manchester with the Mersey, but even when the railways came it still cost Manchester merchants more to move cotton goods from their mills to ships in Liverpool docks than from Liverpool to India or Australia. So in 1887 work began on the Manchester Ship Canal *(pictured left)*. The 36-mile canal took over four years to complete; the first ships sailed from Eastham Locks to Salford on 1st January 1894.

The Mersey ferry Snowdrop was the second boat to steam up the Ship Canal

The Ship Canal begins with the great locks at Eastham (opposite Garston Docks) where vessels leave the tidal Mersey and technically enter the Manchester Dock system. Where the canal passes Ellesmere Port and the huge Stanlow Oil Refinery, the Mersey is at its widest, about three miles across. The Ship Canal and the Mersey are crossed by the road and rail bridges at Runcorn, and above Warrington the Ship Canal actually becomes the Mersey again for the stretch to Irlam, where it diverts from the Mersey to the River Irwell. The two Irlam locks are 600ft long, and take ships up or down 16 feet: the largest step on the ship canal. At Barton the canal goes under the great Barton Bridge, carrying the M60 81 feet up in an elegant arch. Passing the Trafford Centre, the Ship Canal finally reaches Salford Docks and industrial Manchester.

Mersey Ferries' six-hour guided cruises along the Ship Canal have proved staggeringly popular, with two or three trips a month during the summer.

The Leeds-Liverpool Canal is the longest in Britain. Work began on the canal in 1770 and reached Leeds in 1816, but was only connected with the Mersey at Stanley Dock in 1846. 127 miles long, the canal's highest point is 487 feet above sea level, at the mile-long Foulridge Tunnel

Eastham Locks

At the beginning of the 20th century, on both sides of the Mersey estuary were 65 wet docks and 22 dry or graving docks, over 36 miles of quays and 600 acres of dock space

Scouse was a dish called Labskaus or Lobscouse, brought here by Scandinavian and German sailors in the 17th century. It was then salt or corned beef and onions, cooked to rags, mashed up with potatoes and served with pickled cucumber. Over the years it has become a soupy mutton stew served with pickled beetroot or red cabbage

The 2,000-acre Port of Liverpool is handling more tonnage now than ever before and is one of the fastest-growing in Europe. Liverpool is the largest UK importer of grain, the largest exporter of scrap metal, and has been the leading timber port since about 1283. The Freeport is the UK's largest and one of northern Europe's top 10 container ports.

Four hundred years ago, there was no quayside and no harbour wall; the Pool was a natural haven but ships either had to anchor in the Pool, where they'd keel over at low tide, or out in mid-river.

The first quay was built in 1635 while Liverpool was still 'a creek of the port of Chester', and in 1708 local MP Sir Thomas Johnston appointed engineer Thomas Steers to build the first wet dock, opened in 1715.

Progress from then was rapid as Liverpool's shipping trade saw exponential growth. In 1824 the great Jesse Hartley became Liverpool's dock engineer and built the world's first enclosed dock system, allowing ships to move from dock to dock without having to wait for the tide. The vast savings in time and money for ship owners made Liverpool's reputation.

In 1972 the south docks closed to shipping, too small to take container ships. But the north docks thrived; in 1984 Liverpool Freeport opened at Seaforth, and now handles cargoes from more than 80 countries.

Liverpool privateer Humphrey Brooke brought news of the Spanish Armada to Sir Francis Drake

The goods in Liverpool's bonded warehouses on 30 September 1863 included: 1.3 million pounds of cocoa; 1.8 million pounds of coffee; 3.3 million pounds of tea; 5,130 tons of currants; 11,404 tons of molasses; 1.2 million pounds of pepper; 2.5 million gallons of foreign spirits; 1.2 million gallons of wine; 37,512 tons of sugar; 16.7 million pounds of tobacco and 178,007 pounds of cigars and other tobacco products

Although Liverpool had been involved in trade since the Phoenicians sailed into the Mersey, Liverpool's first great entrepreneurs were the privateers. Elizabeth I began the custom of licensing her buccaneers to plunder the vessels of foreign enemies, and Liverpool privateers such as Humphrey Brooke and Fortunatus Wright made a fortune, albeit at great risk.

It wasn't all Liverpool's way; in 1779 St Nicholas's churchyard was fortified with cannon and troops against possible attack from the fearsome American privateer John Paul Jones.

More evidently legitimate trade was flourishing by then; trade with Ireland was already thriving by 1586, and in the mid-1600s many merchants had moved to Liverpool from London to avoid the Dutch and French wars, the Plague, and the Fire of London in 1666.

Privateers were little more than pirates with a royal licence to loot on the high seas

In 1648, the year after Liverpool was made a free port independent of Chester, the town had 24 ships totalling 462 tons and 76 men; a century later the town had 437 vessels.

One Sunday in February 1791, 350 ships sailed out of the port on a single tide. Liverpool was becoming a

Super Lamb Banana,
appropriately sited
outside the chandlers'
Joseph P Lamb

power in world trade. By June 1844 customs revenue for Liverpool for the half-year exceeded £2 million: nearly a quarter of that for the entire British Empire.

One of Liverpool's great trading successes was 'King Cotton'. At first raw cotton came back on the third leg of the triangular trade, bought with profits from slaves sold in America and the West Indies. When the American Civil War put a stop to the transatlantic cotton trade, Liverpool merchants explored the potential for the raw fibre in the East Indies.

Liverpool was the world's centre of the cotton trade well into the 20th century and even today almost 70% of the world's raw cotton for export is still sold under Liverpool arbitration.

Sir Alfred Lewis Jones, head of the Liverpool-based Elder Dempster shipping line, introduced bananas to Britain, although at first sceptical Scousers were hard to convince of the fruit's benefits. The sculpture Super Lamb Banana, *on the dock road at Wapping, harks back to this*

The statue of Christopher Columbus in Sefton Park has the inscription: 'The discoverer of America was the maker of Liverpool'. Liverpool can claim the strongest historical links with America of any British city, from Puritans to the Beatles and beyond.

And most of those links connected from the Mersey. Trade, of course, from 1648 when the first recorded cargo from America was landed in Liverpool; and, shamingly, slavery. The emigration of millions through Liverpool, looking for opportunity in the New World; high profile departures and arrivals, from Oscar Wilde and Charles Dickens to Roy Rogers and Trigger.

Liverpool had the first American Consul in the world: James Maury, appointed by George Washington himself in 1790. A Liverpudlian, in 1776, signed the Declaration of Independence: Robert Morris, born near Dale Street, sailed to America aged 13, and was the master financier of the American Revolution.

The extraordinary story of Liverpool's involvement in America's Civil War can't be squeezed in here; but mention of the Mersey-built Confederate ships *Alabama* and *Florida* is vital. Commissioned by rebel agent James Bulloch, the *Alabama* alone wreaked such havoc amongst Yankee shipping that Britain was forced to pay $15.5 million to the United States in compensation.

When the American Civil War stopped the cotton trade to and from Liverpool, 500,000 workers starved during the Lancashire cotton famine

Buffalo Bill Cody brought his Wild West Show to Liverpool in 1891, with 400 performers including sharp-shooter Little Annie Oakley, Sioux and Cheyenne Indians

The last act of the Civil War was the surrender of rebel ship Shenandoah *to Liverpool's Mayor, 211 days after the Yankees won the war*

Slaves – first white Europeans, then black Africans – were treated as cargo by the traders

By 1800 a quarter of Liverpool's ships were involved in slavery; 10% of outbound tonnage went to Africa to buy slaves

Philanthropists William Rathbone and William Roscoe were among the most vocal in the abolition campaign

The Liverpool road name Goree is after the island of Gorée off the West African coast

The most shaming period of Liverpool's history, with the Mersey at the apex of the triangular trade: from 1700 till 1807 Liverpool ships would sail to Africa with textiles, guns, alcohol, iron; then from Africa with holds crammed with slaves for sale in the West Indies and the southern states of America; returning to Liverpool with cotton, sugar, rum. In the 60 years before abolition, Liverpool was the leading European slave trade port, although as a rule slaves were not brought here. Conditions for slaves on board ship were unspeakable and more than half of the two million taken from Africa either died on the journey or within a few years.

In August 2001 Liverpool saw a ceremony of cleansing and forgiveness performed by African chiefs, after the city formally apologised for its role in slavery.

The Mersey may look west, but ships sailed from here to China, India and all points east from 1834 onwards. The first ship to sail to the East Indies was the *Kingsmill* in 1814, owned by John Gladstone (father of future prime minister William Gladstone); the first Liverpool ship back from China, in 1834, was the Bibby Line ship *Duchess of Clarence* with a cargo of tea and a crew of Chinese sailors - the founders of the oldest Chinese community in Britain.

By 1918 there were 3,200 Chinese men on shore in Liverpool, most connected with seafaring; the community settled around Cleveland Square, Pitt Street and later Nelson Street. Lascar, African and Scandinavian seamen shared the area, and by 1900 the mix of cultures there was so diverse that the local school was nicknamed the League of Nations.

In 1999 Liverpool was twinned with Shanghai to mark the cities' long trading and cultural links

The chief executive of Hong Kong, Tung Chee Hwa, is a graduate of Liverpool University

Liverpool's Chinese Arch – a gift from the city of Shanghai – is the largest outside mainland China

From the earliest days of human habitation in this area, Liverpool has been a place of coming and going. Visitors, traders, invaders and settlers included Romans, Phoenician traders, Saxons, Celts, Vikings - all before 1000AD.

From the late 1600s, when Liverpool began to develop as a port, the world arrived in droves, some to stay, some en route to the New World. Many fled persecution or poverty; others sought their fortune.

By the 1780s the Welsh population of Liverpool was so large that Pall Mall was known as Little Wales; in the 1830s there were enough Scots to support six churches, and two million Irish fleeing the famine came to Liverpool between 1845 and 1855.

The first Jews came to Liverpool in 1740 from the West Indies; later they came from Northern Europe. 4,000 Napoleonic French prisoners were incarcerated here, and when released some stayed. Seafarers washed in and out and built communities.

The Mersey was the key departure point for the New World: between 1830 and 1930 over nine million people sailed from Liverpool to America and Australia in 1,000 ships a year; in 1852 alone 300,000 emigrated. Not all reached their destination. Journeys were grim: in 1847 some 17,500 emigrants (1 in 6) died en route, from disease, shipwreck or fire on board.

In 1851 more than 85,000 Mormons sailed to America from Liverpool, including the father of future outlaw Butch Cassidy

An early emigrant was St Patrick, who is reputed to have preached a sermon in Liverpool before sailing to Ireland in 432AD

Liverpool's population of 20,000 Muslims come from 45 different countries and the city had Britain's first mosque in 1889

Between January and April 1847 alone more than 90,000 Irish arrived here

Woodchurch was the tender for the *Europa* in September 2002

Imagine the Mersey in the 1930s, when Liverpool was at the height of its power and influence, the second port of the British Empire, involved in one seventh of the world's trade. The river and the huge dock system was packed with ships carrying cargoes and people to and from every part of the globe.

This was the home of great shipping lines, including the most famous of today: Cunard. Samuel Cunard, from Halifax, Nova Scotia, founded his company in Liverpool and in 1840 began the world's first regular steamship mail service, from Liverpool to New York; in 1990 Cunard's great liner *QEII* made her first visit to the Mersey, and in 2004 we could see the first visit of Cunard's new *Queen Mary II*.

In 1869 TH Ismay founded the White Star Line in Liverpool; liners renowned for their luxury and comfort and, in the case of the *Mauretania*, their speed. White Star, sadly, is best known for two tragedies: *Titanic*, sunk by an iceberg in 1912, and *Lusitania*, sunk by a German submarine in 1914.

Elder Dempster, T&J Harrison, Papayanni, Booth, Inman, Booker, Lamport & Holt, Canadian Pacific, Blue Funnel, Brocklebank ... great names of the past; the Bibby Line, however, is still in Liverpool; run by Michael Bibby, the sixth generation to carry on the family tradition founded by John Bibby in 1807.

In 1540 Liverpool had 12 ships, totalling 177 tons. In 1937 Cammell Laird launched *HMS Ark Royal* (22,000 tons) into the Mersey.

Ship builders set up in business on this river to supply huge demand from privateers, slavers, whalers, merchants and the Royal Navy. One of the first yards in Liverpool was John Okills, in 1630; by the 1770s, once the first docks were built, Liverpool had several shipyards including Baker & Dawson, Mercer, Rogers & Smallshaw, Fisher, Sutton, and Fearon.

The river's greatest shipbuilding name, however, was that of William Laird, a Scotsman who set up a yard in Birkenhead in 1824; in 1903 the yard merged with Charles Cammell & Co to become Cammell Laird. The last ship launched from Lairds was in 1993; in 2002 the dry dock facility was bought by A&P Group.

In 1840 Thomas Wilson launched the 1,400-ton paddle-steamer United States: *the largest so far built in Liverpool*

In 1857 the screw steamer Pearl *was launched by Lairds on the Mersey for the great explorer Dr David Livingstone, who, with his party, sailed to Africa and up the Zambezi River*

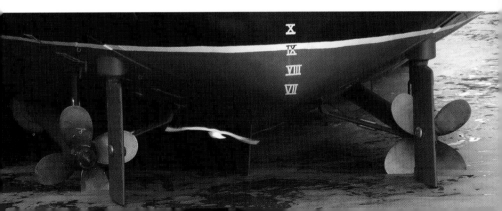

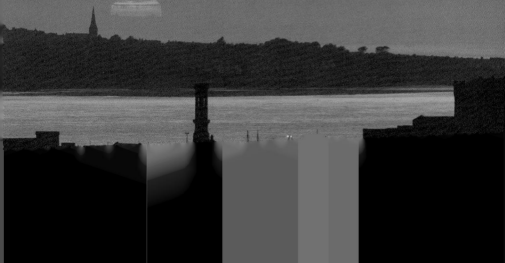

It's ironic how the fortunes of places change. In 1086 the great audit of England's property assets, the Domesday Book, registers Seccum (Seacombe) and Stochestede (Toxteth) but not Liverpool.

The Wirral was a wild and sparsely populated area for long after Liverpool began to thrive; even in 1810 the census shows only 5,000 people living on the Wirral while Liverpool has a population of 75,000. By 1931 the Wirral 310,000 - about the same as today; from a high of 855,000 inhabitants, Liverpool's population fell by almost 50% in the 50 years to 1981.

King John granted Liverpool its first charter in 1207, and Queen Victoria made Liverpool a city in 1880, and between these dates the skyline of both sides of the Mersey has changed quite dramatically with each century; early illustrations and maps look virtually

unrecognisable - in fact the only buildings that remain from the 12th century are the ruins of Birkenhead Priory and Liverpool's parish church, St Nicholas. The original ferry points are lost under concrete and brick now, and there is no visible trace of the old Pool, long since filled in and built over.

While the north docks and Seaforth are active and thriving, from Waterloo Dock south to Herculaneum the docks have been reinvented as housing, recreation, retail, hotels, offices and light industry; some of the buildings have survived, many were destroyed (including the splendid Customs House) in the May Blitz of 1941, and more came down in the 1970s and 1980s. Not all the decisions were good ones, and many local people mourn the loss of favourite places and landmarks such as the Overhead Railway - or the Dockers' Umbrella - which ran seven miles along the river, opening in 1893 and closing in 1956.

There are lots of Liverpools around the world (12 in North America alone), and at least two sit on their own River Merseys (in Nova Scotia and New South Wales)

The first horse races in Liverpool were run along the strand in 1576; races were run over Kirkdale Sands to celebrate Elizabeth I's ascension to the throne in 1588

CAMMELL LAIRD
SHIPBUILDERS ENGINEERS & REPAIRERS

The famous name has gone; the yard
now belongs to the A&P Group

In the 18th century, believe it or not, bathing machines stretched for a mile along Liverpool's North Shore (from the bottom of Water Street); Bootle was a genteel resort of golden sandhills and Everton was a rural retreat for the wealthy.

On the Wirral, the structure most missed by Merseysiders old enough to remember it is the New Brighton Tower; modelled on the Eiffel Tower, New Brighton's version was 567ft 6ins to the top of the flagstaff and when it opened in 1900, it was the tallest structure in Britain. It didn't last; shut during the 1914-18 war, it had to be dismantled in 1921. The brick tower building remained until 1969 when it was destroyed by fire.

In the 19th century, as Liverpool's infrastructure failed to cope with the logarithmic growth in population, the town became one of the unhealthiest in Europe. Anyone who could afford it moved out, to elegant new suburbs south, north - or west, across the river to the Wirral. The Lairds shipyard was growing fast, creating huge numbers of jobs, and Wirral came into its own, spurring the growth of the ferries and half a dozen new terminals to take people to and fro across the Mersey to work and to play.

In 1561 there were only seven inhabited streets in Liverpool: Chapel, Water, Tithebarn, Castle, Dale, High and Old Hall Streets

Where Liverpool castle stood in the 13th century are now the QEII Law Courts

On 10 July 1827 Manchester man Matthew Vipond and Liverpool man Dr Bedale made a wager on a race; they swam from Queen's Dock up the Mersey to Runcorn. The doctor won by about half a mile, in three hours 35 minutes. A rather cleaner river, then.

The best and only vantage point from which to view Liverpool's magnificent waterfront is the middle of the river. The city has always looked outwards to the world, and welcomes those who come from the sea: whether they are homeward bound or visiting for the first time. Whether the Liver Birds are gleaming in the sun or shrouded in sea mist, the sight of one of the world's most famous waterfronts seen from the deck of the world's most famous ferry is an experience that never palls.

In the pages that follow are some of the sights you can see from the ferry, and a listing of the important landmarks, beginning at the river mouth and travelling upstream, south towards Runcorn Bridge and the Manchester Ship Canal.

1 **Seaforth Container Port** Under the blades of the six giant wind turbines, Liverpool Freeport and the thousands of birds in the Nature Reserve live peacefully.

2 **Lighthouse** At the entrance to Gladstone Dock, the light flashes to alert river traffic to ships about to enter or leave the Mersey.

3 **Bootle** Once a favourite seaside resort renowned for its golden sandhills; it was named *Botl* by the Saxons.

4 **North Docks** Include Gladstone, Alexandra, Brocklebank, Canada, Huskisson, Sandon, Wellington, Nelson, Salisbury, Trafalgar; Liverpool's docks are handling more tonnage today than ever before.

5 **Victoria Clock Tower** The hexagonal crenellated brick tower with its six clock faces was built by Jesse Hartley and is known as the Dockers' Clock.

6 **Stanley Dock** The link between the Mersey and the Leeds-Liverpool Canal. On one quayside is Hartley's elegant 1855 Stanley Warehouse, on the other is the 36 acre Tobacco Warehouse: built in 1900 its 24 storeys (12 above ground) consist of 27 million bricks.

7 **Kingsway chimney** The ventilation shaft for the

Kingsway (1971) road tunnel. What look like giant
stereo speakers are huge fans pumping air to the
tunnel below.

8 **Waterloo Warehouse** Now residential apartments,
originally a grain warehouse designed in 1867 by
George Fosbery Lyster; Waterloo Dock itself was built
by Napoleonic prisoners of war.

9 **Bath Street** Named after the public (salt water) baths
here at one time.

10 **Princes Dock** Nine million emigrants embarked here
for the New World; the landing stage was once the
longest floating structure in the world. Now being
redeveloped; the first office building houses global
accountancy firm PricewaterhouseCoopers, whose
founder, Edwin Waterhouse, was born in Liverpool.

11 **Old Hall Street** One of the original seven streets of
Liverpool; key buildings include the brand new
Beetham Towers; No.1 (the HQ of Littlewoods, until
recently the biggest family-owned business in the UK);
the Post & Echo building, home of Liverpool's two
daily newspapers; and the Sandcastle - the nickname
for the Royal & SunAlliance offices (Royal Insurance
was founded here in 1845).

32

12 **Seacat terminal** Landing stage for the Dublin ferry and for the Isle of Man Steam Packet Company ferries.

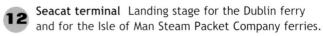

13 **Atlantic Tower** Hotel built in the 1970s, with a shape reminiscent of a ship's prow.

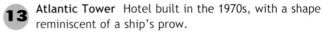

14 **St Nicholas's Church** The church's proper name is Our Lady and St Nicholas with St Anne; it dates back to the 14th century when it replaced the Chapel of St Mary del Quay. The oldest surviving building on the waterfront.

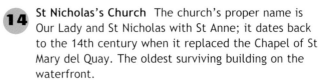

15 **Titanic Memorial** Although the ship's name is not mentioned, the flame-topped obelisk was designed as a memorial to the *Titanic* crew; it is now dedicated to all 'heroes of the engine room' lost at sea.

16 **Tower Buildings** The site of the Tower of Liverpool, built by Sir John Stanley (ancestor of the Earls of Derby) in 1252. It was bought by the town for use as a gaol in 1737 but by 1821 was completely demolished.

17 **Pier Head** Officially George's Pier Head, but George's Dock is long gone, now under the Three Graces. Note the statues and memorials to World War heroes; also the statue of Edward VII, one of Liverpool's four royal equestrian statues.

liver birds

The 18ft high Liver Birds atop the Liver Building are the most famous of these mythical birds, and the renowned symbol of Liverpool. Originally the Eagle of St John the Divine, carrying a sprig of broom, the Liver Bird was the symbol of King John who granted Liverpool its first charter in 1207. Broom, in Latin, is *planta genista* - a pun on King John's family name Plantagenet.

The original seal of Liverpool, carrying the St John's Eagle, was lost during the Civil War in the 1640s; when the seal was remade the bird mysteriously changed to a cormorant carrying a bit of seaweed. Today, ferry passengers can sometimes see live cormorants roosting by the river, holding their wings out to dry, aping their famous copper cousins.

Look for other Liver Birds in the city: over the door of Mersey Chambers and on top of the Walker art gallery

The Liver Bird is at the heart of Liverpool's coat of arms, granted in 1787. The heraldic description is: '...for the crest on a wreath of colours a Cormorant, the wings elevated, in the beak a branch of Laver proper' (laver is a type of seaweed)

The Liver Building's birds were designed by a German, Carl Bartels, who came to England in 1900 but was interned and repatriated at the start of World War 1

18 **The Royal Liver Building** Topped by the Liver Birds, has become the best known landmark on Merseyside. Built by Walter Thomas for Royal Liver Assurance, it is one of the world's first large-scale steel-framed reinforced concrete buildings, a technique that would be used to build the great skyscrapers in America. The largest of the 'Three Graces', opened in 1911.

19 **Water Street** In 2003 voted the fifth most beautiful street in Britain; at the top is Liverpool's exquisite 18th century Town Hall.

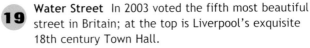

20 **Cunard Building** The latest of the Three Graces; built in 1914 by Willink & Thicknesse as Cunard's HQ, this was modelled on the Farnese Palace in Rome.

21 **Port of Liverpool Building** the earliest of the Three Graces, opened in 1907; designed by Sir Arnold Thornley for the Dock Board, this was said to be a rejected design for the Anglican Cathedral.

22 **George's Dock Building** Built around the ventilation shaft of the 1934 Queensway Tunnel; designed by Herbert Rowse in Egyptian-styled Art Deco elegance.

23 **Albion House** The 'streaky bacon' building, HQ of the White Star Line. Frightened, angry people mobbed the

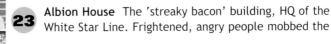

place at reports of the Titanic's sinking in 1914; officials shouted news to the crowd from the balconies.

24 **Mann Island** Site of the controversial Fourth Grace; building is due to begin in the next few years.

25 **Museum of Liverpool Life** In the old Piermaster's House, opened in 1993.

26 **Maritime Museum** Opened in 1980, it includes vessels moored in Canning Dock alongside Hartley Quay.

27 **Tate Gallery** Opened in 1988 as the first branch of the London gallery named after the Liverpool sugar merchant Henry Tate. Designed within the Albert Dock buildings by James Stirling to house 20th century and contemporary art with world-class exhibitions.

28 **Albert Dock** The largest group of Grade I listed buildings in Britain, built by the genius Jesse Hartley and opened by Prince Albert in 1846. Using 23.5 million bricks and 48 miles of beech timber piling, the original construction cost £515,475.8s.1d; restoration in the 1980s cost over £100 million.

29 **The QEII Law Courts** On the site of the old Liverpool Castle, built by King John and pulled down in the

34 1660s, after the Civil War, by order of Charles II.

30 **Chavasse Park** This was the site of South Castle Street, completely flattened during the May Blitz.

31 **Canning Place** Merseyside Police HQ stands on the site of the old Pool and the first Dock; here the old Customs House stood until it was bombed in WW2.

32 **Ropewalks** Wood, Fleet, Seel and Duke Streets were originally long yards where ropemakers would twist great ship's hawsers; later Georgian houses, warehouses and factories. A key regeneration area of the city.

33 **Baltic Fleet** One of the famous dock road pubs - the publican hoists the flag of any Baltic ship in port

34 **Metropolitan (RC) Cathedral** Lutyens' massive 1930s building was stopped by WW2; the cathedral was redesigned by Frederick Gibberd and completed in 1967. Nicknamed Paddy's Wigwam or the Mersey Funnel; noted for its stunning stained glass and the Crown of Thorns on top of the lantern.

35 **St John's Beacon** The studios of Radio City, wrapped round the chimney of St John's Market. The 1960s structure is 450ft high; visitors to the radio studios can clearly feel the beacon sway in the wind.

36 Anglican Cathedral The unmistakable outline on St James Mount, this is the world's largest Anglican cathedral, built between 1904 and 1978; architect Sir Giles Gilbert Scott is buried here. The highest and heaviest peal of bells, the highest Gothic arches, the longest nave, the biggest cathedral organ, etc.

37 Wapping Warehouse By Jesse Hartley; the first of the dock buildings to be converted to residential flats.

38 King's Dock The site for the proposed stadium and arena; the Summer Pops are held here in the Big Top.

39 The Vatican The nickname for the HM Customs & Excise Building straddling Queen's Dock.

40 Cain's Brewery Built by Robert Cain; back in private hands, producing award-winning real ales.

41 Brunswick Dock A highly successful business park and home to HMS Eaglet, the Royal Naval Reserve HQ.

42 Coburg Dock Now includes Liverpool Marina, Liverpool Yacht Club and residential development.

43 **Columbus Quay** Offices and houses on the site of Herculaneum Dock, southernmost of Liverpool's docks.

44 **Otterspool** The name dates back to 1228; in the 1600s it was a Puritan settlement. In the 1940s the Promenade was created using 30 millions tons of land-fill from the Mersey Tunnel; in 1984 it became the International Garden Festival site with its own ferry landing stage.

45 **Grassendale and Cressington** Two Victorian parks of elegant villas; the Esplanade fronts on to the river.

46 **Garston Docks** An ABP port, specialising in short-sea bulk cargoes for industry and agri-business.

47 **Northern Airfield** The old Speke Airport with its Grade II listed 1930s terminal, now a four star hotel.

48 **Speke Hall** A stunning half-timbered manor house built in 1538 for the influential Norris family.

49 **Liverpool John Lennon Airport** The city's fast-grow-ing airport, one of easyJet's key locations.

50 **Hale Lighthouse** No longer in use, this marks the boundary between Merseyside and Cheshire.

A **Perch Rock** The Lighthouse next to the fort was originally a wooden 'perch' erected in 1683. The 90ft granite lighthouse was completed in 1830; its light had a range of 14 miles and was in use until 1973.

B **New Brighton Fort** The Perch Rock Battery, built in 1826 'for the defence of the port'.

C **River View Park** Houses built on the site of the stadium and athletic track in the grounds of the New Brighton Tower - long since demolished.

D **Vale Park** The site of the magazines, where ships would ferry their gunpowder ashore for safe storage before they sailed into port.

E **Egremont** The site of the former ferry terminal in Victorian times.

F **Mother Redcap's** A tavern (now demolished) on Egremont shore. Sailors would leave their wages and prize money with Mother Redcap for safe-keeping; the legend is that a huge unclaimed fortune is hidden somewhere here.

G **Wallasey Town Hall** It was built to face the river, so visitors enter by the back door.

A

M

H Guinea Gap Baths More swimming records have been broken here than in any other pool in the world. Until a few years ago the water used to fill the pools was taken straight from the Mersey.

I Kingsway chimney The other ventilation shaft for the 1971 Kingsway road tunnel.

J Seacombe The clock tower of the ferry terminal has the ferries' radar scanner on top; installed in 1947, this was the first in the world to guide river ferries.

K Birkenhead Docks Entrance to the dock system which stretches inland to Bidston Dock; Morpeth Dock is just to the south, now part of the Twelve Quays ro-ro cargo terminal

L One o'clock gun Still to be seen on top of the small red brick building. Until 1969 the cannon was fired at 1pm daily to allow ships to check their chronometers.

M Queensway chimney The tall Art Deco brick tower (designer: Herbert Rowse) is the ventilation shaft and pumping station for the 1934 Queensway road tunnel, dealing with the exhaust from 40,000 vehicles a day. The twin of the white George's Dock Building.

N   **Woodside**   Birkenhead's ferry terminal; the Victorian visitor centre (the old terminal) is listed.

O   **Birkenhead Park**   Seen in the distance, this park - designed by Joseph Paxton - inspired Ormstead, one of the designers of New York's Central Park.

P   **Birkenhead Town Hall**   Distinguished by its clock tower and green onion dome, the town hall stands in Hamilton Square, one of the finest Victorian squares in Britain.

Q   **Birkenhead Priory**   Founded in 1150, only the ruins remain. Close by is a slipway on the site of the original Monk's Ferry. Look for the spire of St Mary's Church just behind the Priory ruins.

R   **Birkenhead Central Station**   The tower marks one end of the world's first underwater railway tunnel.

S   **Cammell Laird**   Now called A&P, this is the great shipyard founded in 1824 by William Laird and famous for shipping names such as *Alabama, Florida, Mauretania, HMS Ark Royal*, and some of the first steam ferries including *Nun* (built in 1840 and costing just £5,000) and the present *Royal Daffodil*. Cammell Laird launched the last of its 13,00 ships in 1993; since then

it has been a ship repairs and refitters. In 2002 it was bought by A&P Group.

T **Tranmere Beach** Where many great ships came to be broken up, including the Great Eastern, designed by Isambard Kingdom Brunel. The fourth of her six masts (named Thursday) becamse the flagpole of Liverpool FC at Anfield. The skeleton of a shipyard worker was found trapped in her hull.

U **Tranmere Oil Terminal** The great gantry cranes can handle tankers weighing up to 300,000 tonnes; more than 10 million tonnes of oil a year are discharged here and pumped 10 miles to the Stanlow Refinery - the second largest in England.

V **Rock Ferry** The old ferry slipway; the Rock Ferry closed in 1939.

W **New Ferry** A new ferry crossing started here in 1830; it closed in 1922 when a Dutch steamer hit the pier.

X **Eastham Locks** The entrance to the Manchester Ship Canal, and technically the start of the Manchester dock system.

the future

A city never stops evolving; Liverpool has seen some dramatic development in the last ten years, and the next decade promises to be an exciting time when the famous waterfront, the skyline and the whole cityscape will take on a fresh 21st century look.

The skyline is already changing, with the construction of a double tower by Beetham to the north of the Pier Head. The waterfront is due for some notable additions, from further development of Princes Dock to a possible stadium on King's Dock. Most controversial is the so-called Fourth Grace to be built on Mann Island, next to the famous Three Graces at the Pier Head. The radical design chosen has got bouquets and half-bricks hurled in equal measure; time will show if Liverpool still has the courage to make a really bold architectural statement.

The Cloud – Alsop's design for the Fourth Grace

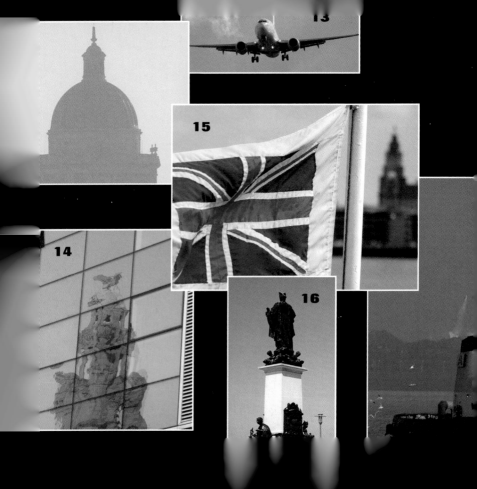

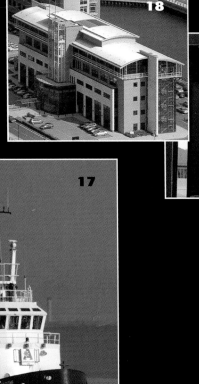

1. The Liverpool Duck, *Whacker Quaker*
2. Canning Half-tide Dock
3. Birkenhead Town Hall
4. St Mary's Church & Birkenhead Priory
5. Queensway chimney
6. Metropolitan Cathedral
7. Riverside Drive
8. The Vatican
9. Tranmere Oil Terminal
10. St John's Beacon
11. Lightship on the East Float
12. Port of Liverpool Building
13. An easyJet 737
14. Beetham Plaza
15. Flag on the Royal Daffodil
16. Memorial to Sir Alfred Lewis Jones
17. The Tug *Gladstone*
18. Princes Dock

Liverpool: the first 1,000 years
by Arabella McIntyre-Brown and Guy Woodland
pub. Garlic Press 2001; ISBN 1 904099-00-9
The key reference book of Liverpool's life and history.
'A must-have book for anyone who loves Liverpool'
240 pages, 200+ full colour photos

A cruise along the Manchester Ship Canal
by Cliff Hayes, pub. Mersey Ferries Ltd; ISBN 0952 6573 17
A detailed guide to the Mersey Ferries' cruise from Pier Head, along the Ship Canal to Salford Keys

Yesterday's Wirral
by Ian Boumphrey, pub. Wirral Books; Tel 0151 608 7611
A series of 10 books; pictorial histories of old Wirral

All at Sea
by Ev Draper, pub. Avid Books 2000; ISBN 1-902964-12-8
Memories of maritime Merseyside

Mersey Ports
by Ian Collard, pub. tempus Publishing 2001; ISBN 0 752421 10 7
Liverpool and Birkenhead

Mersey Ferries carries a full range of books at the Pier Head terminal

Today Mersey Ferries offers you more than ever...

50 minute cruises every day between 10am till 3pm

Morning and evening direct commuter services
with free parking at Seacombe and free coffee on board in the morning

Guided cruises along the 35-mile Manchester Ship Canal
six hour cruises on summer weekends

Party nights with live music cruises
themes from jazz and blues to glam rock

Special day cruises throughout the year
to Liverpool Bay, for river festivals, exploring wildlife

Exclusive charter for your own event

Tel 0151 330 1444
www.merseyferries.co.uk

PROBABLE APPEARANCE OF "SEA GULL" 1822
ONLY DETAIL KNOWN IS THE LENGTH 77 FT

SIR JOHN MOORE 1834

FERRY BOAT ON N
SERVICE 1833

"QUEEN OF BEAUTY" 1845

THOMAS WILSON 1845

GEM 1861

"WATERLILY" AS BUILT 1862
DETAILS FROM BUILDERS MODEL

WATERLILY
FORMER SALOON WAS
ACCOMODATION FOR

"HEATHERBELL" 1863

"MAGGIE" COAL BARGE
1861

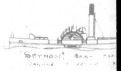

"SEYMOUR" BOAT